CountryLiving

Decorating
with White

Country Living

Decorating with White

EDITED BY GINA HYAMS

HEARST BOOKS

New York

Why White?

When it comes to interiors, white just may be the single most nimble color in the decorating arsenal, ranging from rich, warm shades to ethereal, cool hues. If you look carefully at the undertones, some are blue, others are pink or yellow, and still others are green. The immense variety of shades can feel daunting, but don't worry: no matter which one you choose, it will beautifully complement your interior design, whether it be country romantic, clean and modern, or mid-century classic. And white is more than just a color! It can lighten a dim room and obscure features or play them up, and it's even family friendly—really. Turn the page and see!

Opposite: Casual furnishings outfitted in an array of white shades and a subtle range of pale hues on the walls, ceiling, and trim create a perfect backdrop for this all-white collection of American Art Pottery. Built-in shelves allow the collector to showcase her pieces without cluttering up the space. Arrange like objects together so the repeated shapes have the most impact.

White is Flexible

A room painted white provides light, tranquility, and a sense of spaciousness. And in the blank canvas of that space, endless possibilities can bloom. Unlike so many other colors in the swatch book, a white palette is versatile. A room done up in white may be romantic, rustic, traditional, or contemporary, but it will never become dated because white is timeless.

Left: White projects cosmopolitan polish and panache in this view encompassing the dining room, kitchen, breakfast nook, and a deck beyond. The white walls and ceiling, and floors stained to match the deck outside, unify the space, while seagrass rugs delineate each room.

Opposite: A mix of metal chairs painted with a thin wash of white surrounds a farmhouse table in the kitchen of a renovated barn. The casual multi-layered display of ironstone in various shades of white reinforces the easygoing vibe.

White is Practical

Forget what you've heard: White works great in homes with families. These days, there are white fabrics designed to hold up to sticky hands, panting pets, and wine spills. Faux leather, for example, can be wiped clean with the swipe of a damp cloth. And what could be easier than throwing cotton slipcovers into the washing machine with a bit of bleach? Consider outdoor fabrics, too, which can reside happily—and fuss free—indoors.

Above: This lake house living room is impervious to dampness with its durable outdoor furnishings: a wicker sectional sofa and a weather-resistant rug.

White is Forgiving

A coat of white paint has the magic ability to hide flaws and highlight details, depending on your desire. It can raise the ceiling, open up an awkward space, and create an envelope in which an eclectic array of furnishings can shine. Sometimes, white can even obliterate architectural quirks (so long, shoddy molding) or mask unwanted elements (goodbye, exposed water pipe). Relax—and don't worry about the scuffs on your floors.

Left: White porch paint is an extremely durable choice for floors, and it creates a weathered patina that sings country charm. This compact home office tucked in a staircase landing is practical and airy thanks to the white floor, walls, and ceiling.

White Plays Well with Others

Nothing clashes with white. It allows all colors—from classic navy to screaming neon green—to be seen in the best possible light.

bright idea!
Drape a vintage quilt over the back of a sofa to add instant character.

Left: White couches are a fun place to play with color accents. White will show off your brightest, kookiest throw pillows to perfection. Here, patriotic red, white, and blue details make for a folksy all-American vibe. To pull the look together, the designer started with a large, matched pair at the ends of the sofa and then worked inward with smaller options in similar shades and motifs.

Opposite: Chartreuse walls make a bold statement in a master bathroom outfitted with a gleaming white tub set on a stepped platform. A pair of diaphanous white shower curtains softens the intense walls and the tub's slick surface.

bright idea!

These cabinets had been in this house for more than 100 years. Instead of replacing them, the homeowner called upon white paint and a thorough hardware cleaning for an affordable makeover.

Right: This sunny kitchen, with its painted-white cabinets and walls and charming 1950s white refrigerator, gracefully embraces an array of color accents and textures: lush green foliage in a galvanized tin vase, homemade tree-trunk stools, bright Fiestaware, rustic baskets, and a red-and-silver cart.

Getting White Right

The secret to creating a vibrant white home—whether clean and spare, filled to overflowing with flea-market treasures, or somewhere in between—comes down to one word: variety. Successful white decor strikes several different tactile and visual notes. To design an inviting white room, aim for a combination of hues, texture and layering, patina, and reflective surfaces, as well as a variety of shapes. The result will be warm white style that feels country fresh and livable.

Opposite: Nothing catches the eye quite like the twinkling combination of mirrors and glass. Here a collection of glass bottles used as bud vases lines a white mantel, while the mirror doubles the visual impact of the flowers and amplifies the light.

Hues and Finishes

White can be dramatic and complex. Hues can run the gamut from earthy to icy. Blue undertones make a white feel cool, whereas yellow ones add warmth, and each shade takes on a different cast depending on its finish. Soft whites like cream, ivory, and buttermilk are natural choices for country-style decor schemes. Whites with a hint of blue are great for pairing with modern furnishings. Before committing to a specific hue and finish, paint the wall or other surface and experience the color at different times of day in order to see how the light changes it.

CHOOSING A PAINT FINISH

Here's what you need to know about four main paint finishes.

FLAT PAINT is also known as matte finish and has the least amount of shine. Because it doesn't reflect light, it's the best choice to hide imperfections like bumps or small cracks on walls. It also goes on smoother over rough surfaces, so it's a good option for textured walls. It's a little harder to keep clean, so it's not recommended for high-traffic areas.

EGGSHELL PAINT is the perfect finish for walls. Sometimes called satin finish, eggshell has slightly more luster than a flat finish, but you won't be left with shiny walls. It also resists stains better than flat and can be wiped with a wet rag. Eggshell finishes are often used in bathrooms, kitchens, kids' rooms, and other areas with a lot of wear and tear.

SEMI-GLOSS PAINT is tougher than eggshell, so it will show less wear. It reflects even more light when dry, though, so any imperfections on your walls before you paint will stand out afterward. Semi-gloss stands up the best to water and cleaning, so it's a good choice for a kids' bedroom or bathroom. This finish is also often used for trim, doors, and furniture.

GLOSS PAINT is typically reserved for window and door trim. It's also a great choice for furniture because of its hard and shiny finish. For a glam look, use glossy paint on the walls.

The gentle curves of this rustic hickory and oak armchair and side table draw attention to their imperfect surfaces. The picture frame, made of salvaged wood, adds an additional layer of white-on-white texture to the plank wall.

This family room is a beautiful example of how incorporating a subtle variety of white shades, textures, and shapes can breathe life into a neutral space. Club sofas flank an oversized mid-century coffee table fashioned from iron and bleached oak. A collection of white ironstone china fills the built-in shelves, and aged finds—like a brass candelabra, antique books, and a display of pinned butterflies—lend time-worn elegance.

bright idea!

A built-in ledge, painted the same color as the wall, offers an unobtrusive workstation.

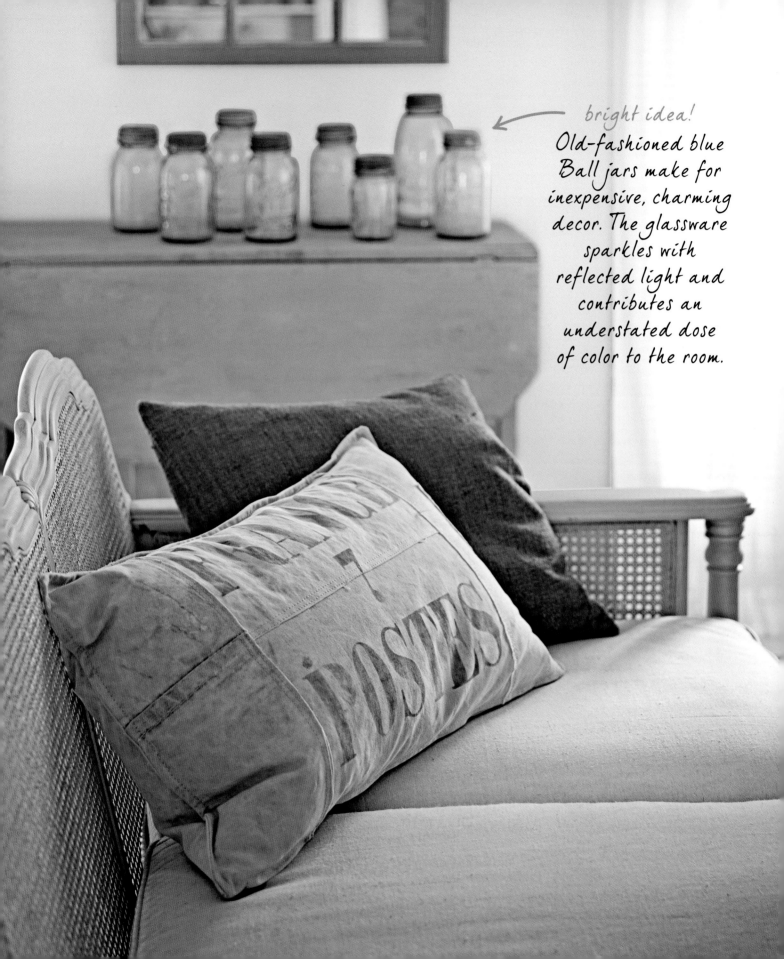

bright idea!
Old-fashioned blue Ball jars make for inexpensive, charming decor. The glassware sparkles with reflected light and contributes an understated dose of color to the room.

Above: A 1920s cane sofa and wingback chair reupholstered on the cheap with hardware-store canvas drop cloths look country chic. Sheer cotton curtains keep the space airy, and the sea-grass rug and bamboo garden lantern strike appealing organic notes. A mirror-front on the wardrobe contributes to the room's serenity by reflecting light and hiding the TV.

Opposite: This simply-adorned living room feels homey because of its comfortable mix of white and off-white shades and finishes. On the sofa, a pillow made from reproduction vintage French grain sacks strikes a rustic note.

bright idea!
Use an antique wood fruit crate to display fishing floats.

Textures and Layering

When the walls, ceiling, and trim in a room are all painted white, the effect can run cold unless the space is filled with pieces that beg to be touched. Look for irresistible textures, such as thick bubble wool blankets, raw linen slipcovers, and gleaming white ceramics.

Above: Wingback chairs upholstered with ticking stripes bring whimsical living room luxury and inviting softness to this breakfast nook. A vintage off-white runner layered on the wooden farm table keeps the scene feeling country.

Opposite: The peaks and valleys created by deep tufts in a rolled-arm side chair and the extensive molding and decorative mantel on the fireplace bring depth to the space. A fluffy area rug, set on top of a larger, tightly woven one, makes the room feel cozy.

Patina

Patina is the beautiful weathered surface that develops on objects over time. A rusted white garden chair, an old-fashioned glass-front cabinet, architectural salvage, well-trod wooden floors—these all soften the stark edges of an all-white interior, giving it a lived-in and well-loved look.

Left: Nature can provide the perfect pale accessories in a white interior. Here, seashells and antique finials rest atop a chest built from weathered scrap lumber.

Opposite: A crackle finish on the putty-colored walls in this entryway is a charming nod to days past.

bright idea!
Mirrors can be stacked
as well as clustered.
Here, the layered treat-
ment draws attention to
the graceful shape and
aged surface of the white
mirror frame.

Left: Almost everything in this bathroom is some shade of white, but the space hardly feels sterile. Rough tumbled tiles, a paint-chipped bench and box, a chest of fourteen drawers, and a thick-framed mirror attract attention.

Opposite: A clean coat of white paint unifies the disparate materials and textures in the kitchen of a Cape Cod–style home—marble, stone flooring, beadboard, and a vertical beam made from a tree.

Shine

White needs reflective surfaces to bounce off and add vibrancy to a space. A collection of glistening glassware, gilded frames, mirrors, lacquer and other high-gloss finishes, mercury glass adds a dash of glamour, a bit of sparkle, and a sense of magic to an all-white room.

Right: Mismatched vintage mirrors in varying shades of white add up to one big statement in a master bathroom.

Right: The eclectic assortment of Indian hand mirrors does double duty by reflecting light in a white room and acting as compositional elements in a charmingly offbeat installation that also includes dog portraits and Belgian wig molds from the 1890s.

bright idea!
Flank a portrait with hand mirrors to scale up the impact of both—creating a whole wall of "art."

Left: Glazed pottery and polished wood can also glow. This collection of turn-of-the-century sock darners made of oak and walnut takes on a sculptural quality when displayed in a shiny white ceramic bowl.

Opposite: In this bathroom, a small mirror and an old dresser in high-gloss paint reflect light.

Opposite: High-gloss penny tile floors, marble-clad walls, and a matching vanity top combine with glowing white walls and bright white trim to create an inviting bathroom.

Above: A brilliantly polished tub reflects light and warms the features of this classic bathroom. Window trim painted to match the walls recedes; furnishings are classic country pieces, with simple lines shown off by solid white fabrics.

Shape

Form takes center stage when using a predominantly white color palette that's free of distracting bright colors and patterns. The particular curve of a table leg, or a floor lamp, the bold lines of a lampshade—the eye goes straight to powerful shapes first, setting the lens through which we experience the rest of the room. Neutral-hued spaces with minimal accessories let the silhouettes of your most beautiful pieces speak for themselves.

Left: In this high-ceilinged room awash in pale paint, a pair of curvaceous chairs command attention.

Opposite: Slipcovered wing-back chairs add interest in a living room bathed floor to ceiling in white.

Right: From the frameless round mirror to the elegant simplicity of the ceramics to the oblong inlays in the drawers of a bureau, this pale dresser-top vignette calls out the geometry of the decor.

Opposite: Set against the white wall, the curves of a glass cloche draw attention to salvaged bottles and feathers and raise them to the level of treasured artifacts.

Chapter
3

Dreamy White Bathtubs and Beds

They are a decorator's strand of pearls. They go with everything, dressed up or dressed down, and are always a chic choice. In the bedroom, the bed itself is typically the largest piece of furniture; when it's white, the effect can be romantic, rustic, or graphic, depending on the style. And no country fantasy is complete without a claw-foot tub. The tranquility of white inspires deeply relaxing bubble baths and the sweetest of dreams.

Opposite: Conventional wisdom dictates white on wainscoting and color above, but here that combination is flipped: the owner painted the trim in her master bathroom mossy green and the upper walls ivory. The result is a cozy corner that seems to hug her vintage tub.

White in Bathrooms

The classic white bathroom fixture is a vintage claw-foot tub. Add plush white towels and bathmats and charming shower curtains for a truly spa-like sanctuary. Reflective white tile, mirrors, and chandeliers make bathrooms feel airy, and pretty countertop accessories, like vintage white pitchers used as flower vases, add personality.

bright idea!
A tall plant stand keeps bath-time necessities within easy reach.

Left: The all-white bathroom of this Maine retreat is punctuated with unique accents, such as a circa-1900 amoeba etching, a cut-paper image of Mao Tse-tung, a pen-and-ink drawing and baroque cast-iron radiator from Architectural Antiques.

Opposite: This master bathroom in a summer beach house is awash in white paint, raising the eave that slopes above a claw-foot tub. A single hydrangea blossom adds a vibrant pop, while an artful display of vintage Chanel No. 5 magazine ads creates interest on what could easily be an overlooked stretch of wall.

bright idea!
To save big on the right lamp, hit the "wrong" department. This outdoor fixture cost just $40 at Lowe's.

Right: Mix modern and classic elements for an unexpected twist. Here a zebra-print ottoman pairs up with a traditional cast-iron tub in the master bath, which is outfitted with white china sinks. The barn door–style mirrors slide open to reveal a recessed medicine cabinet.

CHOOSING A CLAW-FOOT TUB

First manufactured in the United States in the late 19th century, claw-foot tubs remained popular until built-in bathtubs came into favor in the 1930s. Today the freestanding tub is enjoying a revival because of its elegant style and luxurious bathing experience.

GOING VINTAGE Impart authentic old-fashioned style with a vintage claw-foot tub. Check salvage yards, antique shops, and online auction sites for a wide selection. Five-foot-long tubs—the most common at one time—are often cheapest. And a like-new tub commands a higher price than one with scratches or stains, although refinishing can repair superficial damage. Before getting into a bidding war, you should consider the cost of refinishing a tub.

CAST-IRON OR ACRYLIC Traditionalists prefer the look and feel of cast-iron tubs, which can weigh close to 1,000 pounds when filled. If you're refinishing the tub yourself, be prepared. Floors in most homes built to code are able to withstand the poundage. On the other hand, acrylic tubs weigh only 150 to 200 pounds and keep bathwater warmer longer—but are more expensive and harder to find used.

FAUCET Like the supply lines, drain, and overflow, faucets are typically sold separately from the tub. Some are mounted on the tub; others come up from the floor or through the wall. You should consult a plumber to determine which is best, and be prepared to spend as much on hardware as you did on the tub itself.

REFINISHING A like-new tub commands a higher price than one with scratches or stains, but superficial damage can be easily fixed with a few layers of oil-based paint.

bright idea!

This tub cost only $200 at an old fixture emporium. To upgrade it, the homeowner forked over $300 for new chrome supply lines and a European-style hand shower. Worth every cent, these details elevate the whole outfit.

Opposite: Fun vintage finds add interest and color to this white bathroom. The real room-changers in this space are a neon liquor-store sign and an unusual horse rug nabbed at an auction.

Right: Decorative and functional mirrors, along with glass bottles on the windowsill, reflect light in this master bath, while the wooden tray, natural sponge, and fringed bathmat add texture.

Left: The fixed features in this tiny bathroom—tub, sink, and tiled floor—all feature uniformly smooth, cool textures. A simple addition of sweet ruffled shower curtain, a plush bath mat, and luxurious towels add warm layers to the space.

Opposite: This white tub alcove gets its personality from contrasting shapes—the round lip of the tub against the lattice pattern of the windows and straight lines of the built-in ledge—as well as from the contrasting dark hues of the sculptural wooden vase and a funky old stool that holds toiletries.

White in Bedrooms

Textures and layering are the keys to beautiful country white bedrooms. Consider the patina of your bed frame—vintage brass and rustic painted wood are especially beguiling. An all-white bed makes it easy to layer patterns and textures: Pile on pillows of different shapes and sizes and outfit your bed with a variety of soft white linens.

Left: Boasting shades of white in at least four different textiles, including lace, matelassé, and homespun fabrics, this sumptuous monochromatic bed begs to be curled up in.

Opposite: This antique French cast-iron bed sports an array of contrasting textures and pale hues, ranging from crisp white to earthy beige. The sophisticated look is achieved by combining a silky smooth duvet cover, embroidered pillowcases, a knit throw pillow, and a cable-knit blanket. A white teacup lamp sits atop the turned-leg nightstand for an elegant and unusual touch.

Right: Whitewashing the walls in this attic bedroom heightened the drama of its pointed arch, while the blankets and quilts make the open space feel cozy. The fawn hues of the painted floor and the rug are echoed in underside of the bedspread, adding to the sense of cohesion.

Opposite: A chunky knit blanket hangs over the foot of an iron bed dressed in subtle layers of off-white bed linens and pillows. A shaggy rug, layered on top of a smooth one, provides an indulgent layer underfoot.

bright idea!
No need to call the electrician: Simply hang a decorative chandelier from a hook and let the chain double as jewelry.

Opposite: This serene bedroom is the very picture of rugged refinement. Railroad-trestle beams add heft and contrast overhead, while a commanding flea-market oil portrait watches over the antique iron bed.

Top: Old World charm finds fresh life in this comfortable bedroom, where bare floors, simply adorned windows, and white bedding and pillows draw attention to the graceful curves of the circa 1890 Gustavian twin beds.

Opposite: In this romantic bedroom, a sheer canopy tented over a simple white bed lends an ethereal quality. A pile of pastel pillows, punctuated by a single ruffle-trimmed floral version, strikes a sweet, innocent note.

Right: Frothy white bed linens spell romance. Art propped on a radiator and a crystal sconce give this bedroom a sense of easy-going luxury.

This combo bed-bathroom beautifully shows off the pleasures of a roomy tub and a comfy bed. Its serene vibe originates in the beautifully contrasting textures and shades of white, including gleaming porcelain, weathered wood and iron, soft linens, and fresh flowers.

Country Classic:
Blue and White

All-white color schemes are lovely, but don't discount the effect of judicious bursts of color. Blue-and-white is one of the most beloved color combinations in country decor, and it is tremendously versatile. You can combine blues and whites with wild abandon, as nearly all the shades of these versatile colors get along just fine with one another.

Blue can be cozy, cool, tranquil, intense, delicate, and energizing. And there are just as many strategies for integrating blue into your white home: paint, textiles, ceramics, furniture, and more.

Opposite: French terra-cotta pitchers glazed with sprightly stripes and spots, hand-sewn pillows made from Swedish textiles and French tea towels, globes, and book covers bring lovely strokes of blue to this mostly white living room.

Shades of Blue

A blue-and-white palette can be deployed to widely differing effect in any number of combinations and shades—from watery light blue and periwinkle to cobalt and navy—through paint, fabrics, floor coverings, and collections of glass or ceramics. Deep, dark blues give gravity to a room and, depending on the shade of their white partner, can impart a formal or casual vibe. Pale, whispering blues suggest simplicity and serenity, making it ideal for bathrooms and bedrooms. Vibrant blues make for especially cheerful kitchens, whether used sparingly through accessories against an all-white backdrop or more boldly on the walls or cabinets themselves.

Left: Ocean-blue linoleum gives this seaside cottage kitchen a vibrant nautical feel, echoed in a collection of oyster plates displayed on the wall. The reflective quality of the high-gloss white walls makes the room feel especially bright.

Opposite: A document box from the late 19th century now serves as a trunk for extra blankets in this guest bedroom. Old pharmacy bottles and a Shaker box echo the blue hue in a harmonous arrangement.

This homeowner opted for a charming reversal of the typical scheme of white cabinets and blue walls. A soft blue-gray adorns the cabinetry and island, while a coat of white paint transforms the rush-seat stools. A collection of white bowls displayed atop the cupboards, lusterware on a shelf above the stove, and a variety of white platters displayed in recessed shelves makes for pleasing variety throughout the room.

Opposite: The renovated kitchen in a farmhouse built in the early 1900s retains the charm of the era with a mix of stone and wood countertops. The bright blue walls frame open white shelves stacked with dishes and glassware in a limited color palette—all the better to maintain visual order. Guests can help themselves to dishes—and empty the dishwasher—without having to guess where things belong. The woven cotton rug conveys the look of checkerboard linoleum or vinyl flooring, a tradition in many country kitchens, without the commitment of living with it indefinitely.

Above Left: In this bedroom under an eave, pale blue walls, a white ceiling, and an iron bed refreshed with white paint create the calm framework that allows other colors (the black frames) and shapes (the bedside table) to stand out with three-dimensional intensity. The window, left unadorned to let in a maximum of light, acts as decoration in its own right.

Above Right: A minty-blue wall showcases this collection of white vases to beautiful effect, while the curvaceous blue hardwood side tables provide an additional pop of color.

This sparsely furnished space benefits greatly from
the blue-and-white scheme. White paint from rafter
to floorboards calms what could be visual chaos,
while the inclusion of the dusky blue antique chest
continues the color scheme of the rooms beyond
and creates a quiet focal point.

Furniture and Dishes

Blue-and-white accessories abound, from Wedgwood and antique Chinese export porcelain to splatterware and spongeware to off-the-shelf plates. Adhering to a consistent blue-and-white palette keeps it all compatible. And don't forget the furniture: Slipcovers are a practical, versatile way to change things up.

Left: A high-low mix of cobalt ceramics—boasting a variety of patterns and prices—creates an effortless tablescape that really cooks.

Opposite: A wall decorated with old shutters imbues this dining room with personality, while careful use of white softens the look and gives it a natural ease. The pale rug and white wooden dining table keep the busy space from feeling cluttered, and the airy white-paneled curtains open up the room.

bright idea!
Extend the length of store-bought
white drapes, and avoid dirty
hems, by sewing dark borders to
the bottoms of white curtains.

Opposite: Bold, clear colors add instant charm to any all-white kitchen. Here, crisply striped stools and enamelware in primary colors give the room a casual, friendly feel.

Right: Grouped blue-and-white china draws the eye up in this slick, spacious kitchen. Coordinating blue-and-white accessories, including the area rugs, kitchen towels, and enamelware, tie the space together.

Textiles

A blue-and-white theme can be introduced with fabrics through upholstery, rugs, tea towels, bedspreads, and curtains. The ultimate mix masters, blue and white make it easy to pile on patterns.

Left: Golden floors glow in a soaring space made cozy by a built-in daybed adorned with blue-and-white cushions sewn from table linens. The painted blue trunk, a flea-market find, adds a rustic texture to the mix.

Opposite: Floral fabrics come in many forms, from loose and blowsy to positively graphic. Here, mix-and-match cushion covers beautifully demonstrate that blue-and-white textile patterns allow you to play with a wide range of sizes and hues and easily create a unified effect.

bright idea!
Wall-mounted bulkhead lights take the place of beside lamps in tight quarters.

Right: In this California kids' room, navy bedspreads and a chevron rug suggest "nautical" without going overboard.

Opposite: Old-fashioned? Not these florals. Coax yourself out of hibernation with garden-fresh bedding—paired here with stripes for an unexpected combination.

bright idea!
Loosen up a traditional
bedroom with mis-
matched quilts.

bright idea!
White frames unite and elevate paint-by-numbers art.

Opposite: Century-old quilts in Pinwheel (left) and Bear's Paw patterns dress these antique wrought-iron beds, the different patterns linked by their common blue-and-white palette. A hand woven rag rug in similar tones adds folksy texture underfoot.

Above: In tidy contrast to the bright collection of vintage prints clustered above, the Adirondack beds in this kids' room are outfitted in classic country style with crisp white bedspreads accented with blue-and-white striped wool trading blankets and rustic plaid pillows.

Left: The pinstripe pattern on the navy blanket adorning the foot of this white bed mirrors the tongue-and-groove planks that line the master bedroom walls and cover the headboard, which conceals a closet.

Opposite: A little royal blue goes a long way in this restful guest room. A solid cotton canvas shade cuts a bold swath across a pair of windows set in a bright white wall. The effect is repeated with a striped pillow on the simply dressed bed.

Color Accents on White

The lining of a curtain, a pair of pillows, a throw, a collection of ceramics—punches of color can change the personality of a white room faster than you can fill a vase with flowers. White rooms are among the most versatile, as they provide endless opportunities to effortlessly redecorate. The beauty of a white room is that it reflects light unlike any other color and, as a result, allows accent hues to truly pop. With the mere addition of a few colorful plates to open kitchen shelves, you can transform a cool white room into an inviting space, while a bright blanket adds warm welcome to a pale living room.

Opposite: Bold, bright, and unexpected, citron-yellow garden chairs glow against a dining table draped in exuberant ruffles.

Kitchens and Dining Rooms

The beauty of choosing accent colors for all-white rooms is that you can experiment with bold hues without expending tons of time and effort—and what could be more fun than that? For your kitchen, hit the farmers' market or produce aisle. Apples, pears, lemons, or other citrus add natural brightness to a pure-white kitchen. In a dining room, swapping out table linens, slipcovers, curtains, or even chairs are all simple ways to work color into an all-white scheme.

Right: Drape a quilt over a railing to lend a shot of color and pattern to the landing, and enjoy a cheerful greeting every time you climb the stairs.

Opposite: Committing to color in the kitchen can be as simple—and effective—as storing pots and pans where they can be seen. Stainless steel and marble look snazzy paired with fire-engine red cookware and a trio of green ceramic bowls filled with fruit.

FEED THE BIRDS

bright idea!
Boat hardware takes
on a supporting role as
kitchen cabinet latches.

Opposite: Black Windsor stools and a bright red-and-white rug surprise in this kitchen. Rugs are an eye-catching and a low-commitment way to introduce color into a white room.

Left: With the exception of the late 1700s beams, the Vermont homeowner started from scratch with this kitchen, transforming the space with custom cabinetry, counters from locally quarried Danby marble, and a refurbished 1950s stove.

Opposite: Because they're all white, these mismatched porcelain pieces read as a set; the collection really pops against the distressed blue-green finish of a 19th-century cabinet.

Right: Handsome kitchen islands can add a note of color to an otherwise white kitchen, and they don't have to cost a fortune. This rustic green Mexican desk, which was scored for $350 at an antiques shop, now serves as a one-of-a-kind workstation in this white kitchen. To make the piece even more functional, the homeowner improvised a lower shelf by propping basic wood planks atop the stretchers.

Opposite: The variety of rustic whites in various shades and textures, punctuated by delicate pink accents, adds up to a charming dining room.

Above: Teal cushions and bright blue throw pillows jazz up this breakfast nook. The table is constructed of salvaged wood, and the unexpected mix of aged texture and modern color, together with the pristine white lines of the benches and walls, gives this family space unique appeal.

Bedrooms and Living Spaces

A touch as subtle as a colorful monogram on a pillow, a bright lampshade, or a bold throw rug instantly adds character and depth to a space. Colorful artwork, decorative pillows, fresh flowers, shelves filled with vibrant pottery—even the spines of books in a bookcase—can infuse a white room with color.

Left: A quilt made of recycled saris brightens this cozy bedroom.

Opposite: A mixture of red-and-white toile and ticking linens softens a wrought-iron bed in this Prince Edward Island beach house. Patterns don't have to match to work in a white room— they just need to be pleasing.

Opposite: This 1748 New York cottage was crafted from a salvaged schooner. A 1950s Eastern European runner patterned with subtle stripes graces the striking white mezzanine with a splash of subdued color.

Right: Hats, bags, and hoodies are all corralled on one wall of the foyer in this Prince Edward Island home. The red wooden bench adds a jolt of color, as does the vintage lobster sign, which also contributes the spirit of the coastal location.

Left: Subtle color accents also mix beautifully with white. Here, a handsome silver-gray throw on a linen-upholstered bed picks up the cast of a Venetian cut-glass mirror from the 1920s.

Opposite: Taking your cues from nature guarantees a successful blend of color with white. A soft palette of dune yellow and sky blue blends seamlessly with the view from this seaside cottage.

bright idea!
Liven up traditional pieces with playful accessories. Here a 19th-century Masonic hat and a golf-tee necklace lend levity to a formal bust.

Opposite: Bright accent colors and rough-and-ready elements, like a folding iron cot with a feed-sack bolster, add essential energy to this rustic master bedroom, which would otherwise be dominated by the stately four-poster.

Right: Lilacs, irises, and lupines invigorate a 1930s Haeger urn.

Black, White, and Bold

The truth may rarely be black and white, but when it comes to interiors, there's no debating the infallibility of the pairing. The bold combination is timeless and transformative. Pretty much every room can benefit from a touch of black, and in spaces awash in white, black's grounding quality adds sophistication and drama.

Pay special attention to shapes and lines, as both take center stage with this pleasing color combination. Treat black furniture like sculpture; silhouetted against a light backdrop, each piece can make a statement. Walls painted stark white or a soft ivory provide the perfect canvas for photographs and artwork presented in black or white frames. Contrasting textures are important, too—think velvet, glass, metal, mohair, lace, corduroy, and distressed surfaces.

Opposite: This freestanding pine hutch, dating from the 1800s, delivers both storage and a dramatic place to show off white ceramics.

Walls

With a black-and-white color scheme, you can go forth with a spirit of adventure, knowing that whatever your choices—regardless of provenance—they will match. Black-and-white checkerboard floors are synonymous with classic country interiors, while slick, all black underfoot is traditionally associated with loft living. Either floor treatment can add drama to contemporary *or* country spaces. Want something with even more flourish? Of all the ways to incorporate black into a decorating scheme, perhaps the bravest is by putting the bold hue on the walls. Dressing vertical surfaces in black and white can infuse even the most mundane room with elegance and beauty.

Above: Black chalkboard paint yields a changeable canvas in this powder room. The knob on the door is real, but the lyrical "wallpaper" and the wainscoting are drawn with chalk.

Opposite: Walls and trim painted high-gloss ebony throw the white shapes of the 1950s furniture into sharp relief in this cozily mysterious living room.

Above: Black-and-white-striped upholstered walls create a dramatic backdrop in this two-toned room. The golden warmth of the paintings and wood dresser offset the intensity.

Opposite: The crisp combination of charcoal black and bright white in the entryway provides the equestrian homeowner a setting that anchors this collection of paintings, photos, prints, and ribbons. Different textures—wainscoting, velvet, brass—soften the space.

Opposite: Use wallpaper paste and a flat sealant to transform newspaper into wallpaper. A stack of 1960s Ukrainian newspapers scored at a flea market lends quirky panache to the walls and ceiling of a small bathroom.

Right: An old black-and-white train sign brings focus to a creamy white-painted wall hung with an artful jumble of prints framed in unifying black.

Furniture and Accessories

The power of black is especially potent when it's used with a piece of furniture. A black chair, bed, settee, or table becomes far more than a functional piece in a room. Set against a white background, dark silhouettes shine. On a smaller scale, such as with accessories, a minimal palette makes it easy to pile on patterns; the secret to success is varying the size of the prints.

Left: This white mud-room gains dynamism from the touches of black: the bureau knobs, painted wooden chair, checkerboard pillow, striped mug, picture frame, and even the black edges of the Wellies.

Opposite: Black Windsor chairs, slat-backed benches, and sleek wrought-iron chandeliers stand out like line drawings in this dining area painted with high-gloss white walls and dramatic gray-black trim.

Opposite: On these living room shelves the soothing black-and-white theme unifies a quirky collection of vintage cameras, ceramics, and glass bottles, using white vellum-covered books and black hardbacks as risers.

Left: Beautiful black-and-white photographs casually displayed with pushpins and binder clips yield a certain effortless glamour. A stack of coffee table books, most of which have black covers, reinforces the low-key perfection.

Left: Dark furnishings and accessories help ground and define white spaces. Painted black stools, along with dark-walnut floors and green soapstone counters, center this white kitchen.

Opposite: Black antique brass fixtures cut a striking silhouette in this airy breakfast room.

bright idea!
Turning a fabric's "wrong side" faceup, as the designer did here, can reveal the subtler print of a bold pattern.

Opposite: Nothing updates a cane-back chair quite like a geometric black-and-white print. In an office furnished with flea-market finds in a range of whites, the lattice-patterned fabric stands out in crisp relief against the gently peeling pieces.

Above Left: Washable canvas slipcovers—one white, one deep charcoal—flanking a jet-black stove atop easy-to-mop white painted pine floors make for a kid- and dog-friendly living room.

Above Right: Boldly contrasting stripes can serve as a dramatic element, but in this family room black-and-white ticking has a playful feel.

White and Wood

White pairs with wood in a natural, sometimes rustic, aesthetic that may be casual, sophisticated, or both. In even the most lavishly wood-clad rooms, a generous dose of white immediately brightens the space, infusing it with light and air. Conversely, an all-white interior can be warmed by a few wood accents and will show off any wood furnishings in fine relief.

If a home features exposed wood posts, or unpainted moldings, railings, or similar architectural elements, they can frame a white wall. Exposed beams and rafters may highlight the ceiling with a geometric pattern. To decorate effectively with these elements, be mindful of the contours, volume, textures, and hues of the furnishings you choose.

Opposite: This refreshingly rustic bathroom keeps things simple—white towels stored in a basket beneath the basin sink, toiletries decanted into glass containers, and a bouquet of fresh-cut wildflowers displayed in a white enamel coffee pot. The sink support is made of fir.

Post and Beam

Timber-framed homes, both old and new, often feature exposed skeletons that add distinctive personality to the spaces they enclose. Simple white decor offers a good balance to their warm, usually rustic, rhythm.

Right: White stain allows the knotty pine to show through on the walls and ceiling in this 1850s farmhouse, adding a subtle texture that softens the massive post and beam. The coffee table—rustic boards topping an old chicken crate—repeats the hue of the frame and pulls together the white furnishings, which are accented by taupe stripes, the side-table base, and iron lanterns in the background.

Opposite: The hallway of this 160-year-old farmhouse features an exposed post, brace, and beam, and a similarly rustic ladder (which leads to a sleeping loft). A white faux bois mirror and vintage bench with a worn finish, topped with a couple of pale pillows, are the only furnishings needed.

A sense of simplicity infuses an upstate New York home with spare white walls. The living-dining area is decorated with a mix of wood furnishings, including Indonesian rush-back loungers and an antique American farm table with cane-seat chairs.

Right: Sunshine streaming in through a tall window bounces off a bed covered head to footboard in loose-fitting white linens. Set in a glorious envelope of walls, ceiling, and floor clad in burnished planks, the effect is warm and comforting.

Opposite: An iron bed frame offers a delicate counterpoint to the stronger beams and uprights and softens the peninsula effect of the white bed against the dark wood floor.

Wood in White Kitchens

Anyone who loves a white kitchen but finds all white a tad chilly will appreciate the warmth that wood can add. The reverse is true too: Add something white to brighten wood cabinetry, like shelves filled with white dishes, and the room will sing.

Left: Light-colored wood like this bamboo counter adds warmth without weight to a white kitchen. A few wood bowls and some terra-cotta pots similarly accent these creamy cabinets.

Opposite: Wood countertops are utilitarian and relatively inexpensive, and offer a pleasing change of pace in an all-white kitchen and a homey backdrop for showing off white accessories.

An antique butcher block, open shelving, and suspended potrack all lend rustic comfort to this bright farmhouse kitchen.

bright idea!
Instead of doors, try using skirted curtains on rods to hide below-countertop storage.

Above Left: A kitchen without upper cabinets looks and feels spacious, but the expanse of wall just begs to be adorned in some other fashion. What could be more appropriate than a collection of wood cutting boards, hung with their diverse shapes silhouetted against the white?

Above Right: Dark-colored base cabinets sit comfortably on a dark wood floor. Here the double tier of upper cabinets is done in white on a white-tile wall. The contrasting effect is handsome and not at all overwhelming.

bright idea!
*Kick-pleated cotton
duck skirts dress
up barstools.*

Lots of white makes a kitchen pretty and bright.
The addition of a luxurious expanse of cherry wood
atop this large island softens its mass and keeps it
dressy. Slipcovered stools and the ornate pendant
light are elegant enhancements.

Right: An old mirror makes an intriguing backdrop to a collection of tiny white creamers that sit on a honey-toned wood counter. The mirror's weathered, driftwood-colored frame and pearly surface give the little pitchers context; without it they'd be lost and out of scale against the blank white wall.

Wood and White Accessories

Wood can play a chameleon role against white accessories, dressing them up or down to enhance the style at hand. Rustic planks, elegant vanities, mirror frames (plain or fancy), and small accessories are among the options to mix with white tile, marble, paint, and porcelain fixtures.

Left: An antique pine cupboard aged to the color of maple syrup centers attention on a collection of white ironstone vessels, setting off their individual contours as well as their impact as a group.

Left: The bold red interior of this circa 1870 cupboard makes a dramatic backdrop for a dazzling collection of white ironstone china.

Opposite: A vintage wooden baker's rack serves as a beautiful venue to store and show off dishes.

The White Stuff: Displaying Collections

How do you make an artful asset out of your beloved momentos? When they're predominantly white, the trick is to make them stand out—as individuals and as a group. One of the easiest and most effective ways to display pieces is to cluster them together rather than scatter them around a room. Try to put treasures to work; if vintage collections or contemporary ceramics are your thing don't let them just sit there. Stack your beloved items like sculpture—and fill them with off-season or extra goods such as flannel sheets, summer shoes, and winter gloves.

Opposite: No cabinet space deep enough to hold platters? A custom rack solves the problem—and offers up a pretty, practical way to display a handsome assortment of shapes and sizes.

Left: There's not an open nook or cranny in this wall-spanning white cabinet, but a sense of order reigns. Like pieces are arranged next to each other, and spaced evenly apart on the cream-colored shelves.

Opposite: Freewheeling displays of all-white objects can be charming. Here English ironstone and Chicago-made Red Cliff pottery in a wide variety of shapes and sizes are shown to beautiful effect against the contrasting dark gray interior of a built-in kitchen cabinet.

bright idea!
A plate rack set in a kitchen island offers stealthy storage.

Opposite: Think vertical as well as horizontal when showing collections of platters, and take advantage of unexpected spaces. Sides of kitchen islands rigged with plate racks can be prime display areas.

Right: Elegant pieces don't need fancy dressing to stand out. In this home, simple white shelves against a white wall focus attention on the various shapes and pale hues of the arrangement of English Staffordshire ironstone and American stoneware.

Opposite: The open shelving makes the most of the small kitchen's pitched ceiling. Even with the jumble of objects, the room doesn't feel cramped because most everything stored on the shelves is white—even the stand mixer.

Right: This kitchen takes a radical approach to storage by putting everything on view. Floor-to-ceiling shelves, made accessible by a rolling ladder, hold an amazing array of white tableware.

Small Objects, Big Impact

Collections tend to evolve; adopt a flexible framework for arranging them so you can easily rotate pieces in and out. Picture ledges allow you to swap out mirrors and paintings effortlessly. Also, take advantage of vertical space.

In any house, there are only so many tabletops on which to showcase knick-knacks. So if you tend to amass large numbers of small collectibles, consider climbing the walls, as in the room shown on the opposite page.

Above: Three white plates imprinted with a lace motif look stunning against this Tiffany blue wall and echo the white floor, lampshade, and details on the chair.

Opposite: This white cuckoo clock pops against a taupe wall, while a collection of white ceramics adds interest on a ledge near the ceiling.

Left: Stoneware cast with real sweaters lends unexpected texture to a collection of white ceramics.

Opposite: A hallway coatrack becomes a creative composition of safari hats and photographs.

bright idea!
Stacked under a glass cloche, even simple skeins of yarn resemble sculpture.

Photo Credits

Lucas Allen: 5, 15, 24, 25, 66-67, 76, 120, 121, 126, 135, 136, 152

Christopher Baker: 72, 77, 79

Kindra Clineff (Terry John Woods, stylist): 39, 70-71

Jonn Coolidge: 30, 87

Grey Crawford: 60-61, 127, 138

Roger Davies: 7 (top), 31, 51, 107, 116

Miki Duisterhof: 34, 50, 58, 84, 86, 110, 159

Philip Ficks / Homeowners, Jesse James and Kostas Anagnopoulos, of Aesthetic Movement: 26, 49, 94, 122-123, 128-129, 141

Don Freeman: 99, 155

Dana Gallagher: 13, 69 (left), 108, 117 (left)

Gridley + Graves: 65, 75, 80, 157

Alec Hemer: 10, 98, 105, 111, 142, 143, 151

Aimee Herring: 74, 133, 149

Ray Kachatorian: 92

Keller + Keller: 83

Max Kim-Bee: 12, 22-23, 36, 44, 88, 100, 101, 104, 114, 115, 139, 140, 153

Michael Luppino: 38, 59, 131, 149

Charles Maraia: 18

Kate Mathis: 144

Andrew McCaul: 40, 55

Andrew McCaul and Catherine Gratwicke: 27

James Merrell: 130 (left)

Laura Moss: 7 (middle), 28, 32, 45, 68

Victoria Pearson: 78, 93, 112

José Picayo: 69 (right)

Steven Randazzo: 57, 134

Lara Robby: 4 (top left), 146

Lisa Romerein: 16-17, 91

Keith Scott Morton: 37, 106, 177 (right), 124, 125, 130 (right)

Tim Street-Porter: 33, 62, 96

Robin Stubbert: 11, 29, 52, 109, 147

John Valiant: 35

Mikkel Vang: 46, 82

William Waldron: 64, 81

Björn Wallander: 4, 6, 8, 14, 21, 42, 48, 54, 56, 73, 89, 90, 95, 97, 102, 113, 118, 145, 158

Julian Wass: 132

Andrea Wyner: 2, 7 (bottom), 41, 53, 150, 154

FRONT COVER: iStockphoto
BACK COVER (from left): Andrea Wyner, Kate Mathis, Andrea Wyner

Index

Note: Page numbers in *italics* indicate photograph captions. Related photograph might be on opposite page.

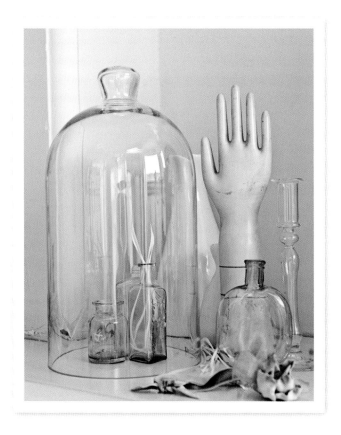

HEARST BOOKS
New York

An Imprint of Sterling Publishing
387 Park Avenue South
New York, NY 10016

Country Living is a registered trademark of Hearst Communications, Inc.

Every effort has been made to ensure that all the information in this book is accurate. However, due to differing conditions, tools, and individual skills, the publisher cannot be responsible for any injuries, losses, and/or other damages that may result from the use of the information in this book.

ISBN 978-1-58816-860-3

Library of Congress Cataloging-in-Publication Data

Hyams, Gina.
  Country living decorating with white / Gina Hyams.
      pages cm
  ISBN 978-1-58816-860-3
  1. White in interior decoration. I. Country living (New York, N.Y.) II. Title. III. Title: Decorating with white.
  NK2115.5.C6H93 2013
  747'.94--dc23
                                                                    2012027227

Distributed in Canada by Sterling Publishing
c/o Canadian Manda Group, 165 Dufferin Street
Toronto, Ontario, Canada M6K 3H6
Distributed in the United Kingdom by GMC Distribution Services
Castle Place, 166 High Street, Lewes, East Sussex, England BN7 1XU
Distributed in Australia by Capricorn Link (Australia) Pty. Ltd.
P.O. Box 704, Windsor, NSW 2756, Australia

For information about custom editions, special sales, and premium and corporate purchases, please contact Sterling Special Sales at 800-805-5489 or specialsales@sterlingpublishing.com.

Manufactured in China

2 4 6 8 10 9 7 5 3 1

www.sterlingpublishing.com